The Lion and the Golden Calf

by Ronda Eller

EBIP

SkyWing Press,
37 91 2 Jenkins Rd., RR2 Clinton, ON N0M 1 L0

skywingpress@gmail.com

ISBN-1 3 : 987-0-9809335-0-5

Library and Archives Canada Cataloguing in Publication

Eller, Ronda L., 1 965-
    The Lion and the Golden Calf by Ronda Eller

Index.
Poems.   978
ISBN-1 3 : ~~987~~-0-9809335-0-5

        I. Title.

PS8559.L5424L55 2008   C811'.54   C2008-900575-9

 cover illustration by Ronda Wicks.
title page illustration by Ronda Wicks

Previous Publications by Ronda Eller

My Harmonic Perfection, HMS Press   1994
Whale Songs in the Aurora Borealis, HMS Press   2004

Poems in this Collection that have been singly published:

'Tooth on Tooth', The Innisfree Poetry Journal, USA 2006

'White Crimson', The Innisfree Poetry Journal, USA 2006

'Pulled From that Spindled Track', Labour of Love Literary Journal, Toronto, Ontario, Summer 2008

'For Closure', Labour of Love LiteraryJournal, Toronto, Ontario, Summer 2008

Table of Contents

Solstice of Friendship

The moon's round face glows brightly
within the sky,
the glowing face of friendship
frames you and I

and on this earthly canvas
we call our home
our friendship finds its solstice—
becoming full.

The sky was made for holding
the radiant moon
and friendship made for bonding
me to you.

Inward Sky

Listen to your spirit sing
   — hush now, hush now—
let the quiet calm come in.

   Bathe your soul in gentle rain
      — silent, silent—
   feel the cleansing, shed old skin.

      Fix your sight on inward sky
         — focus, focus—
      let the clouds clear from your eye.

Feel your aura glowing tall
   — sense it, sense it—
beacon-hands on heaven's wall.

   Pro-grade to the moon and sun
      — balance, balance—
   love and logic dance as one.

      Listen to your spirit sing
         — hush now, hush now—
      let the quiet calm come in.

Down To The Shore Now

I will go down to the shore now
with tears trickled down to my toes
where the cold, rolling surf will co-mingle
and listen to their woeful heartbreak-tale
then wash them out to sea.

I will go down to the shore now
where sun will eclipse me- void of colour
so none may view my desolate shade;
the cool breeze will whisper comfort
into the ears of my dying soul.

I will go down to the shore now
and watch birds of prey feed on young salmon
and I will remember how life can be cruel;
how love sometimes fails to live a full life
or grow old gracefully.

I will go down to the shore now
where grief can pass unnoticed
and I'll take a red rose and a daffodil.
I will float them on waves with your edge-worn photo
attached by a string

and I will trust the waters to offer them up
to an unfamiliar land only dreams remember;
a place I know I must soon go
if only for youngsters who tell me so-
because the lower tide
                    must also break!

Au Courant

Night molecules -
light, buoyant ethers of dream -
skip and glisten inside shadows
where thoughts break away
and time, like a silver globe,
turns its other cheek
to listen.

Telepathic chambers -
lilting, cosmic voices of eternity -
bounce and echo between walls
of primary neuro-cell receptors
where I break away
and visions, gold dust slivers,
bare sharp, glistening teeth
to speak.

Au courant -
the lucid imprint of tidology -
branded, embedded in human psyche
where bicameral minds slip away
and I, like quicksilver's draft,
feel the essence of a kiss
and pray!

Ripple

These are the days of my despair,
when darkness hangs
its gloomy veil about me,
chanting in unfamiliar voices,
(radical phrases) while I cannot
find my easy chair in the corner.
It is not there.

I sit at the center
of the kitchen's cold linoleum
smashing dishes (already broken).
This is the summer of my discontent -
assigned to me while choices
were seeds sleeping in pockets of gods
and I was merely a ripple
in the water of life.

White Crimson

The inventor, for the invented, gambled
his life on a pen, his heart on a stage
where the dancer danced or pretended and ambled
out, weighing himself on the thread of a page
    that reemed at life for being incomprehensible.

He mused over women, both baroque and refined,
growing awkwardly taller but not thin in nerve;
still determining marriage the finish line
to romantic endeavours and courting words-
    undeceived by the wrinkles in his aging pen.

The poet, adrift on a platitude, painted
pictures that spiritually twisted about
envisioning a pure infiltration of blatant
inscriptions in quiet volumes— the shout
    of a Harpy impaled on the crimson tide!

Still, the white bird whistled with rose under wing,
one eye jammed tight-shut from blowing sand
where his talon had dug up some truth and the thing's
two-handed wisdom could imprint vision's brand
    on the broken-heart ensign of inchoate man.

Inventing wings on which to fly
near an earth-rooted tree that sheltered him
he gambled his death on ethereal sky
and waited to hear the midnight clock's chime—
    both eyes shut tight,   both eyes open wide.

Pulled from that Spindled Track

i.

In shades we shape and shift 'though light flows 'round,
not knowing where we'll be, who we'll become,
some greet the sky and some bend t'ward the ground;
believe each quest to be the final one

but gyres twist and turn then call us back,
bare clothes reworked, made new with threads of gold
brought through the gap, pulled from that spindled track
through bleary infant eyes, soon to grow old.

ii.

Darwin sculpted apish evolution,
Heraclitus taught that our souls self-unfold
Jung claimed that ego forms in revolution
as trait meets situation, is unfurled.

These schools of thought were taught to me in childhood
when I cared not to think of soul's deep measure
but search, instead, for faeries in the deep woods
and dream the dreams all youngsters dream with pleasure.

iii.

In shades we shift 'though light comes flowing 'round
and chase our scarecrow days through vast life-fields,
slipped forward on a gyre that makes no sound,
when, in hindsight then, we see our dance revealed

but even then the characters keep changing
and music agilmente ends up as largo
the crescendos rise and fall, keep rearranging
the dancer and the dance— so on we go.

She Speaks to Him of Perfect Union

Sad soul, that breaks upon the rocks of time
and longs for rest in arms along the shore
where uttering lips may speak of nothing more
arrested in the breach, so, left behind.

May you, in places time can't comprehend
see your heart's desire to make its peace;
'though all the glittery starlight there must cease
and all ambitions must give up their hand.

No lover there to want, no pain to hold
for lovers all are blended in the tide;
a perfect state of mind fulfilled inside
the banking of a spirit bright and bold.

No currency for entrance at the pass
or labouring soul achievements to remit;
'though bound in time their measures don't submit
to any law such perfect union has.

Oh soul that drifts through moods on open sea
and harbours all it hopes in undertow
may you and I surrender all we know
in placid bays that time cannot conceive!

The Unzipped Valentine

Out of Chaos came Desire
and now, O fullest of moons,
your timely arrival expedites lunacy
in Eros' charted, annual insurgency.

Like good mortals we, the simple,
plimmed by a strange Olympian urge
shield our Psyche from Love's wrath
and rise with Eros, returning
to our roots-   and what effect
will your Selenian heart make of this?

What consequence will
your power boost spawn
while Eros' passion-laced tip
spews forth his/our unzipped libido?

Raped by an arrow's prick
from the babe disguised
as on his mother's mission,
we- whose Psyche has been kept
secure within the castle- this year
we quiver...

                    this year we wait...

Breast-High Day

Summer spanned full
cooked in breast-high day
and on the barbecue, sauteed,
we celebrate the earth
and the sun's
most radiant inflourescence—
fullest light blooming
more distantly,
a sampling most eloquent
from the humble bracht
at Solstice

Raging Tides

What changes in the raging tides of time?
A house falls down and then another built
surrendering children to its open fields
once scorched and left as fallow- now grown fine!

See in children's eyes more worlds unfurled,
raw-spun upon the wheel of incarnations
emitting static from charged imagination-
new visions sewn in this boy or that girl?

Inside time's gyres a country rises, falls
while peace and war are hedged like child's play
religions subdivide amid forays
caught on would-be spindles meant for all.

When marriage vows decry that death will part
the fiber of a love that's been engendered,
we must believe that love will be surrendered
by fateful gyres that breed eternal hearts.

So do the Muses spin amused, no doubt,
ensuring souls become enmeshed as one,
returning to the source where they'd begun
and, with their composites, are then spun out.

What changes when the tides let go of time?
A life felled down concurrently is built
through surrendered spirits in a cosmic field
always waning fallow- ever born in soul and mind!

The Lamentations of Isis

O Thoth, O Wisdom: Where's my lover now?
I do not see him, looking west to east.
I do not see him, looking north to south.
Where may I find his hands to soothe my breast,
and where, his lips, to taste upon my mouth?

Osiris- brother, husband, lover, friend-
as kite I fly the mountains peak to peak
and torture mindless sea-life for a clue
yet, this time, empty-handed, empty beaked
of a hollow heartbeat's hope in finding you!

O Seth, O Jealous: See what you have done?
Osiris has become a deity
and for all the tears I wept to give him life
each time you rose to kill him, lovingly
I drew him back- you'll never have his wife!

Osiris- brother, husband, lover, friend-
I, your goddess Isis, pine for you;
I ache to feel the heat of your embrace
as, life to life, you see each mortal through
and I- cling to the memory of your face.

Armageddon's Bride

Wisdom perches on a tower
shouting at pedestrians.
She stands against the dark grey sky
heavily laden with summer rains.

Her tiny white feet, same hue as her gown,
touch lightly on the rooftop
making no attempt at self-camouflage
preferring to draw all vision up.

She is the bride of Armageddon-
the crimson knight who will set her free;
whose slate black horse will charge and trample
all foolish wandering on the street.

In hailing her ice and snowy heritage
her flowing train flags in the wind,
so she'll be hailed on his arrival
and with his passion in hand - ascend.

To gain her wisdom through his touch
she waits to greet his consummation,
knowing she'll rise as a golden lotus
in the reign of Armageddon's nation!

Song of the Mulberry Children

Here we come like weeping saints-
mulberry children ringing with tears,
dew drops falling from the petal's veins
before dissipation by the sun-mutineer.

Here we come like faeries dancing-
parasols raised in a grand cabaret
at the Folles-Bergeres with all its prancing;
summoned through the gaze of a golden stag!

When we arrive how will you know us?
Our white will be laced through with lavender,
our bodies pale as melted snowflakes,
and our scent pre-blended with the air.

Here we come, your merry visions-
each one fettered by ball and chains,
martyrs lanced by your incisions
trajected through those stiff-necked veins!

Rebirth at Uisneach

We worm through the tunnel at Uisneach
   slithering to scale our own passage
     inside Eri's birth canal;
trying our Spirit's hand at its own rebirth
where feet have become
                 ungrounded.

   From her humble womb
we grope through fleshy Darkness
having no choice but to move forward
   knowing that what Earth holds mute
   her heart steals in
          to whisper.

We witness Time as a clever matron
who sweeps the truth of her own genesis
          away from the threshold
yet, despite her effort, we
  somehow remember.

In recreating our first crossing
her cold, well-worn landscape
winnows us away from the home Fire
    but in the resurfacing we drink
the Light of our own afterbirth,
    seek a new Stone of Divisions
    and begin...
             again.

Awash

We pass like days dissolving
in the tides of time, unsalted—
without preservation of mind,
without reservation, unaltered,
our spirits collapse by design
without love nor ever resolving
any need or yet a longing
that came in an earthly body
or that could ever come again.
We drift within the remedy
that carries us at body's end;
our spirits awash and responding
to the merfolk beckoning.

Ibyss Song

To the ibis on the beach
parading in front of me:

I saw that shifty head cocking:
cotton ball and mask
stuffed into its flaccid straw
end of a snaky white neck
covered in seed-gone dandelion
and pulling a fur-feathered
    white / gold egg—
shape of a prancing body

flaunting pregnant ownership
of sacred hidden mysteries
ready to bubble up in the hatchway
and drop out right there
before me.

You feigned not to know
I was lurking in the reeds,
behind my dark lens and shutter,
but I was convinced your exhibition
had already wed its audience
long before it took my stage.

Who could miss that ruddy red
beak of a slivered harvest moon
slicing the air like a conductor's wand,
or perhaps, a wizard's...
while performing a head-tossing ritual
of metered chants
& overtures?

Who could argue
that your same-tinged limbs—
gnarly thin bleeding effigies
of mistletoe blighted mesquite—

declared less
than death defiance
          throughout the ages?

What trickery
to leave me haunted
my Olympus yielding
paper icons
seduced by the whispering
of your cold abyss eye—
          never caught.

Shadows In the City of Brotherly Love

They wait for me

like the Baptist John in Philadelphia
ready to cast me a cold blackened eye;
right hand outstretched, pointing to heaven,
inducting me into a new order; left hand,
alas, focused downward- condemning me.

Rodin must have felt their presence too
as with plaster cast he poured a head
and forged out his soul in heated bronze;
calling up old John to be reborn.
What merriment he must have found
when he chose to reveal John naked;

a truly unabashed Christian forerunner
or perhaps the Emperor deceived
by his fine new clothes. The deviance/trickery?
away from social norms put clearly on display
in the "City of Brotherly Love" where,

across the aisle lay that same dark face
stuck on a platter- smoothly glossed depiction
of beheaded misfortune; cold eye gazing upward
at nothing. The Hand of God is nearby too—
busy at molding something undefinable
while outside, The Thinker, sits high on his pedestal.

Around the corner, The Gates of Hell wait
to tower over me in antiquated green patina.
In visiting this meandering collective
I think of poor Rodin who was initially refused
studies in art, aborted pursuit of religious vocation,
rejected in military service for being short-sighted

and I wonder of his potential achievements
had his road been clear, straightforward, how

 did he relate to John and where
will martyrdom find its next end—
    or beginning—

how to traverse or evade
this labyrinth of shadows; echoing
soliloquies.

They wait for me.

She Echoes from Grave to Grave

I.

What ecstacy may be found in the echo of a whimper
that clings to the nun as if in a ceremony
bought with the rapture of her own accord
and there, on the altar of highest ordination,
has lain her heart to rest sublimely with the Almighty
when, in fact, her muse did carry its eyes from grave
to grave and there, in a moment of true revelation
began to understand the familiarity of towers;
steeples that climb ever-skyward, like Babel's
befouled attempt at inclusive sanctification,
held in seclusion by the rushing in of splintered tongues-
or lives that could not, together, carry a single composition
no less aspire toward heavenly orchestrations?
Where, in this flaming cloister of gyres
should Blessed Hildegard be found if not in meditation
where, blind as she often was and all the world can be,
she still lifts her voice in praise of a Master
that she is wont to see?

II.

What anchor reveals the strength of its metal
then gives way
when, after seceding its lifetime to prayer
and the vigilant mooring of mankind's impure vessel,
be shorn away by some dark arm of death
and embalmed with ambiguity in some strange place?
I say, that in a vision delivered during youth,
the anchorite was wedged and still imposing
holy will on the unruly tide though, being steadfast,
she was unaware that the ships had all, but few,
forgotten her and in her continuing labour remained
tethered to the voice of a Master
that she, as yet, was wont to know.

III.

Flailing her arms in the tides of time
this virgin of ecclesiastic faith rippled through
speaking in a foreign language somehow understood
by a simple, tithing child who, emerging
from an ancient corridor of Light, would dare not
trample the monastery in fun or disregard
but would, perhaps in time, be suffered
to break the chains of bondage worn around its neck.
What religion may be promoted or endorsed
by saints as this- who cannot find eternal rest
            above/below
a physically impassioned world that first responds
with insults marked on the ends of rapiers?
With missiles aimed skyward like Babel towers
to splinter eyes where sight cannot be stolen
and, blasting open grave to grave, pleads
for forgiveness in the name of "Holy Peace"
that it might choose to claim as Master
if upon the earth itself, it was not wont to see...
or know.

Witch of the Caves

In the Cheddar caves
the old witch still dances,
well lived beyond her years
and that mangy old dog,
her decrepit companion,
we smell him still,
snoozing by the hard-boiling cauldron.

Days peel away from these
sooty subterranean walls
and fall in ancient, flaky coats
on our shoulders. We gasp
in the torchlight that draws us
into the cavity— deeper—

farther than the hanging stalactites
that paint themselves
among shadowy alcoves,
suckling tears and mimicking
dragons that once threw their own fire
here—

         here—

where tiny newts burst
beyond the fervent flame,
springing into great monstrosities,
wide-eyed for breakfast
but then, and even now we know,
   no more!

Loneliness permeates
this dim ice-dropping plaza.

We sense its reeking emotion
turned away,

the unholy burial of an outcast,
frozen solid in rock,
the slowing down of seasons passing,
the top spinning out over time,
bewitched—

       an old woman,
her swollen, unshod foot
snagged
and abandoned,
misunderstood but still
in some mysterious way,

dancing.

Indivisible

Softly, the night
and you
in sleeping shadows breathe
unscalable... as mountain peaks-
snow white omnipotence
crowned in the moment
of your almost being, here
a god, unfettered
through dreamy emancipation;
indivisible and right.

Breasted, the night
holds you
like the Madonna revering
her magnificent love spawn,
serenaded by angels on a breeze-
their light cherub fingers
gently dancing inside
my window dress, whispering
magi secrets
to the candle's flame,
kissing faint billows
of frankincense and myrrh

while...

my starlit mind, the night
hums along
in spiders' silent weaving
a self-crucificial lullabye
painfully emended
to exact
your weeping return
from Bethlehem.

Come My Lover

I.
Come my lover,
come to me...

from the womb you've been
drawn and challenged
to seek what rest resides
upon earth's bosom.
You've learned to murmur
recitations of your own rising
up from dust
with sated-folklore-belly
burgeoning with wisdom
and unclaimed miracles...
disallowed the rite
of growing old.
I know the lesson
of your fall from sky
into the magmatic core-
human... and no less a god
flame that entered
this tragic circle
consuming its head
with its own tail,
resurrecting itself only
to spiral again.
Come my lover,
come to me...

since there is nowhere
else to go.

come to me...

II.
Come my lover,
come to me...

lie down inside night's quiet cradle
and bathe me with your lips' sweet nectar,
let our spirits dance, co-mingle,
embedded by rhapsodic splendour.

impose your bare-breast chest on mine
so we can beat as one, supine,
and harvest each reverberant echo
between us— leaving none astray.

Come my lover,
come to me...

before the morning lifts its lids
and tries to catch us with its glare,
let's weave a consummate spirit-blanket
of our reunion, repose there.

come to me...

III.

Come my lover,
come to me ...

our wind-struck bonds have been cast off
and all that we once knew is gone—
the days have turned upon their heels
and left us with emancipation.

There is no need to question why
some precepts live and others die
or how the wind derives its breath,

how love lives on beyond its death
to thrive where thieves and beggars fall
we've seen it and lived through it all.

Come my lover,
come to me...

the air is ripe for blending
these currents we're ascending,
these spirits we've pretended
to own as ours, contended
once as independent
when freedom thrived
as a mere vision.

Come my lover,
come to me...

so when the daylight finally breaks
we'll dispel flesh and bone heartaches
and rise... revived together!

come to me...

Enlightenment

The scraped bone of destiny rises and bubbles up
beyond the surface as, with water-logged blue eyes,
disbelieving, we fall into it, over it, becoming young
children struck and impaled by cold, rape-happy rocks-
stopped for the first time to wonder if we finally are
at last beyond the required shape for innocent repair.

The assaulting heat in each flesh-searing throb
does not really burn through the insult as deeply
as it does through the labouring, enlightened pupil
flooding painful tears into Nibiru-dark pools
of ancestral oceans, swimming our skeletons
to saline dense shores where we finally emerge-

absorbed in crisp granules of sand bleaching white
in cradle-rocked tides of old blood, asking how
our destiny became so intrinsically grounded.

The Alliance or,
The Double Vision of Michael Robartes Made Full

She emerges through silence
    in pre-dawn haze-
eyes yawning for a gulp of air
    to hasten
            her reawakening.

Indeed,
            not even Yeats
would know her un-engendered face
full of shell-pocked crevices
    peering at him
            in the moon's 28th phase.

    And she...
his coveted woman's breast,
    animal he'd longed to tame...
kindly assumes the male demeanour
            assigned her
when caught in a double vision
yet holds her head high
    with daft inattention.

Her lioness form,
cast off,   reclines
in sand-smacked simplicity
    that dismisses poetic nostalgia
in a successful alliance
between both

Animus
    and Spiritus Mundi

while his Buddha sits erect;
    finally surrendered
        of all its love-sad tears.

She rises as the dancing girl
  and yet the poet-gods continue
      their underground banter
oblivious to her foolish grin
      as,

  in an opportune moment,
she soft-pedals her way

              toward the East.

The Lion and the Golden Calf: A Vision

The eye, still haunting sleep
looks down upon a sun-bronzed lion,
hungry for Shangri-La or Zion,
lurking within a psyche's deep

vision- oh vision of immortal genesis,
where gods play for the King of Kings...
Whose lips' broad grin glowed wing to wing
and recruited that old Saul of Tarsus?

That same eye rigid, vacant, blind,
keeps visiting by day and night
to prey on what preconscious sight
one barely can afford or find

yet Buddha, brisk in meditation
while the young girl dances like a fool,
mulls over each befuddled rule
aware her calf's regeneration

   will also feed the slouching beast.

Autumn Friendship Prayer

At my table may there be
a horn of plenty set for thee,
laid out on crystal ware to bring
health-blessed seeds for spring planting.
May your senses yet be kissed
by the sweetest smell of amethyst
floated by orange candle mist.
I give to you this corn husk doll
that represents my heart and soul
to have and hold as, friend to friend,
we walk together through this land.

Escarpment of a Thousand Dreams

Each sleep contains a thousand dreams
and in each dream a thousand plays unravel
for a thousand critics past, present and future.
Each past one holds a thousand gavels
in hands that reach a thousand graves;
their opinions, mixed and mottled echoes,
haunt a thousand current contemplations.
Each present critic flaunts a thousand words
review of what each episode could mean
but never settles one, just prattling on,
throwing chaos into the full-minded broth.
Like mimes the thousand future critics gesture,
flagging hands and shirking pasty-faced
while laughing like a thousand mockingbirds
just waiting to come to life—
to be awakened.

Twilight Snow

At twilight, the fresh-dropping snow
glitters topaz, or perhaps amber,
under the town's street lights—
danger yellow of a honeybee jacket,
crime scene barrier tape,
an intersection light
meant to slow travellers to a stop.
  Stop.
    Consider the eerie view:
Beyond the first few cold-eye breaths
you can warm up to it. You can
hear its silent sighing as it lies
intently staring back (so human-like)
at the great sky
from which it fell.

The Henges' Kiss

I.

Lead me to the wood-rot rings
to seek myself in water and earth
and prepare for yet another birth
because the spring is calling me
to stir from this deep stony sleep—
Lead me to the wood-rot rings!

Let the ents that live here know
the earth has drawn me from its soil
to live upon its back and toil
that I, its humble servant might
resume my passage through its Light—
Let the ents that live here know.

Let me kiss these timbered feet
and hear the birds at planting time
call out the fruit that will be mine
as, from the henge I go and sow
new life to dress this naked stone—
Oh, let me kiss these timbered feet!

II.

Lead me to the stony circle
so fire and air can make their claim,
my bones consumed by the high priest's flame
because I have seen death and can
fly, breathless, through its eye again—
Lead me to the stony circle!

Let centuries erode the henge,
its calendar gone but will once more
rebuild itself in other form
and, though its altar pales from view

its palm still yearns for the day it's due—
Let centuries erode the henge!

Let me kiss those sarsen stones
where fore-bearing spirits wait within,
I see their faces all agrin,
they murmur with everlasting voice
already keening on my choice:
Oh let me kiss those sarsen stones!

III.

From woody henge the cursus calls
and as I grow I know I'll follow
meandering past hill and barrow
where living history keeps sensation
in the boned remains of civilization—
That from woody henge the cursus call.

Along the Ave. to Slaughter Stone
I pace the breadth of summer passing,
entranced by voices everlasting.
I fall to cold and wintry sleep
that feigns no charm but no deceit
along the Ave. to Slaughter Stone.

From life to death to life I pass,
wood to stone in body, then in spirit
from stone to wood— and I revere it:
the cycle that goes on like seasons
never questioning for reasons
as from death to life to death I pass.

Ecdysiast

In an amatory grin
there is an illusive elixir simmering;
an ecdysiast smothering
beneath too many clothes,
effulgent skin at center stage
under edacious eyes
that cast a lover's torchlight—
illuminating the bedroom's private eclat.

What such emissive grin reveals
in gracile accolades
must be the mystic dancer's art-
disrobed within the dance!

Rock-a-Bye

pendulum and grave—
                    rock-a-bye,
        'bye,
                'bye—
life's sway   death's way

the lull of silence
ticking
                through earth
red worm slithering
eating dirt   sinew
        from which it came—

from which it grows
it goes
        mute as ever, the same
tail weaving
left—   right—

obscure passing of grit
                    blackened night
six feet below the edge
of fright;
                    weaving right
weaving left—

pendulum and grave
both deaf
                    to spirit song
where soul sings high

"Rock-a-bye baby"—
            Rock-a-bye
        'bye
                'bye.

On Being Asked for
a Dream Journal Preface

Leave the phlox at my bedside stand
that I can hide it 'neath my pillow
when deep slumber dons its priest-dark robes
and passes round the offering plate,
collecting up my dreams as tithes. Oh,
leave the phlox at my bedside stand
to stow some savoury ort for morn!

The Genius and The Beast

It wasn't the statue of the man
that made me smile
but the politics behind it-

as if molding his effigy in marble
would contain his spirit
and console the people
that their demon was dead;
that forward-thinking governments
would do their own improved-thinking
henceforth...
after playing down the genius.

The general public was to remember him
as an advocate for power and control,
suppression of rights and dignities.
Bittersweet-that, he never had the power
to prove himself a military analyst
instead of a beastly advocate
for wanton extirpation.

He would not be remembered
for prison time and years in exile
for the crime of government
changes beyond his control...
nor remembered
as a man who loved women
almost more than politics itself,
a Valentino in his own time;

the writer of love poems
and comic tragedies
ever dodging or else suffering
cupid's ambush...

through letters and desire
or that his wife and five children
pined for him; expressing love
to have him with them
in safety.

It wasn't the statue of the man
that made me smile
but how the end
had justified the means:

'The Prince', was molded there
in his marbled hand;
it seemed the government
had learned from his text well.
It was, ironically, better
to be feared than loved
in the Florence of his day
and they made his name
synonymous with the demons
they dared not face...

poor Old Nick
feared into infamy-
and how entirely
Machiavellian!

Her Final Coming of Age

She rocks in the chair
and waits—
grey woman in a grey room,
steely hairpins neatly buried
in chimney soot
-like, flax-tight tresses
that frizzle,
fade&fizzle
out
in the backdrop
of an alabastrian face,
her abandoned desert—
ideal place
for an eye storm
brawling beneath
cumulonimbus brows.
She seems
an angry specter—
her loneliness near
transparency
but for intaglio lines,
wrinkles fleshed
through her pores by time
screaming of intrusion—
a Real life scaled,
caught up on the reel,
coughing
on the swollen fullness
of its own mouth
while I
can only look
and bite my tongue.

Catch Weed

Catch weed of life:

The world- a bright red rose
sometimes turned to spike the leg
of a near passerby

who responds in sharp

with chords pulled tight
to rail at brambled rudeness.

The mind- its own briar
patched over,   fibrinogen hiding
the still tender surface
of earth, a fetid consciousness;

the dust that formed an eye
not meant to look down on pain
or see where it had been.

The heart- a fertile forest
found sometimes heaving
for lack of a canopy
and growth-

so thick that all's a struggle

as the soft skin bleeds dry
in the bed below,
shrugs off chaff
and sharpens

in its own brilliance.

These Woods Are Mine

In stopping by woods on snowy evening
I am at home; these woods are mine.

Here, a skeletal tree line sidles up
to my footpath. Like a twisting and snapping
chorus line, it whispers quiet-toned responses
to winter's slow and steady breath. It draws—
yawning in strange shadows across the soft,
white carapacial canvas that waits
for the hunkering down, the crunching
under my sole's infixion as I plod along
toward my log house. Deer have etched out
scuffy, hoof-prints in paths a few yards off
and tracked out a maze where cottontails
have played a game of hopscotch in my absence.

Everything around seems to dance through silence
like an old spinster having learned to savour
the natural security of her own independance,
neither lonely nor deceived by hibernal pond fish,
vacant bird houses or any tiger lily's abandoned shell.
She witnesses the dead, interred amongst the living,
and prepares herself to welcome every spring's rebirth.

In stopping by woods on snowy evening
I know the presence of both Jack and Robert
Frost paradoxically rapt in winter's embrace
creating, dismantling and creating anew;
how they write on my window singly handed,
no more dead in spirit than life itself,
tracing their way through snowbound nights
while I settle in to doze by the fiery hearth
because these are my woods, my snowy evening,
and I have no more promises to keep—

I am at home.

50

Tamarack

You stand tall—
a sky-piercing treetop,
having needled your way into winter
through shades of ochre—
refusing to part with summer attire;
merely changing it
with hopes of appeasing
the cold maiden

and now
snow weighs heavily
on your feather-soft boughs.

I see you slump
under the burden of that...
and those precious cones that you,
in your deciduous resolve,
refused to offer up
to the wind's sweeping hand.

I can almost hear you sigh
as you shelter them,
almost see your slow-sapping tears
beginning to flow; we both know
that you will keep them
but a little longer
and they will leave the nest soon—

motherhood's fruit
        departure-ripened.

On the Mezzanine

On the mezzanine
our effigies
grip passes and programs;
bone and flesh fused
in rising heat.

Our eyes fan inward
to center stage
where lovers bewail
separation's anguish
and we, with them,
                  fly further
from ourselves.

Tragedy
whimpers and mewls
inside hearts creasing
under a weighted quest
for one last
terminal
sigh ...

Hell's ambush finally jars,
screaming delight
through tortured catgut—
defiance under skillful fingers
swarms the pit below
then gapes wide ...

our spirits pale
and shift to prey!

Night Subterfuge

Found in strings— threaded night
bursting through the subterfuge
pulled, twitching musculature
in the quiet rustle-about of atrophic leaves
stuck, shrivelled on the limb;
their dander raised to dissonance
by the barky brush of air
hissing its voice, careening
across the fields, playing broken
corn stalks— old woodwind reeds.
Never a peaceful moment
not orchestrated...
waiting under the bow
for the listener
to listen.

Ninety-Two Years of Wisdom

The clear night sky
brings out too many stars tonight
where clouds should be casting themselves
after news of your passing.

I wonder how they dare
to betray my sense of loss
with bright twinkling ... joyous
laughter but, then again,
you always knew
how to clear the clouds away,
finding the bright, tidy sky
whenever set upon
by the stormiest ocean.

'No need to search for grief' I say—
you say. 'Enough of that
in the world without inviting it'.
'Everything lives in transition.'
Your ninety-two years of wisdom,
your full life embraces me,
coddling me back
into subjectivity.

The clear night sky
brings out too many stars tonight
eager to embrace you
embracing me— both grandmother
and granddaughter—
peaceful—   still.

(for my grandmother, Hannah Marjorie Wicks, nee Broadhurst
who died August 17, 2007; one of the most beautiful, God-fearing,
God-loving women I have ever known)

Ritual

Lushness of basswood—
the beauty of its bracts
perfectly balanced—
adorned by heart-shaped leaves,
greening, graceful punctuation
for a poker-faced blue sky.
The curious sunlight flirts with her
in golden rays deflected
through ballerina toes, twirling
 lightly over a spread
of dainty, yellow flowerettes
as they blossom pale submission
to spring's passionate musing.
Her pistils bursting forward
with ruby fullness; tender swelling
erections surrounded by dancing stamen,
blushing red maidens
performing
their own fertility ritual.
Quizzical, this natural grace—
that in spring she cannot see
her own grandeur, nor
her barren winter desolation
yet she carries on
and I am, as ever, called
to sit by her feet
and sing.

For Closure

The ink washes down, pooling
by the freshly dug grave
and I, in my quest for closure,
hold the shovel steady, ready
to dig deeper— not to study
dirt, dust or the ashes that made me
but to know the comfort being sewn
into a bed like the one where I
will eventually lie. My pen
must know how to write for the future,
to cleanse itself with the salty eye-stream
of mourning, turn up the nitric sod
that contrives decomposition
until it mulches into fertile loam
that will feed my soul
through the coming slumber
and sprout fresh lilies
by the pool.

Grog

Floated in a hiccup of conscious thought
a lover's atman is near-glimpsed- then gone
as a talon of night incises my heart,
extracts its desire for other vistas.

In that eternal space I deposit a trail
of supplicant moaning for a resurrection
along the same path to that exact place
to revisit that hiccup and lover revealed

but morning refuses to dawn the same twice
except for that filmy grog of the mouth,
that pasted swallow of re-immersion
I know so well to be compromised.

Floated in a cup of peppermint rinse,
an astringent for loneliness chuffs and is gone
as daytime floods my desert heartland
and harnesses me to its daft chain gang!

Recalcitrant Corner

Pawed by something fat
    and lazy
isolation
stares at me
with green
     crepuscular eyes;
a lonely refugee
of my tenth
   California Smoothie
curls up to sleep in my lap,
       purring presumptions
of a new soul mate
   discovered within
my dark, recalcitrant corner.

   Even alone,
my densely rod eyes can see
      that I am not.

The Miser's End

I asked myself if I should date again,
to spend my heart and soul on one more man,
the miser held his coins close to his chest
"How much can you afford my pretty friend?"
I wandered through the plaza, looked around
at couples hand-in-hand that I had found,
the miser held his coins close to his chest
"Three fifths fall out of love by the fifth round".

I went to search for answers in the field,
debating love aloud to grazing cows,
the miser held his coins close to his chest
"your gamble may make pain the final yield".
I found a priest, a man of holy cloth
to ask if spirits should all be betrothed,
the miser held his coins close to his chest
"Forget the priest, he took a celibate oath".

A brothel was the next place I would see,
the girls drank cups of men but were not free,
the miser held his coins close to his chest
"Though sex abounds here, where's security?"
In widowhood, my spoon seemed rather bent-
what heaven would call back the heaven-sent?
the miser held his coins close to his chest
"My money lasts beyond your investment."

I asked myself if I should date again
while sitting with my friend on his deathbed,
the miser held his coins close to his chest
the coins fell asunder in the end.

Tooth-on-Tooth

We've lined our journals with walked-on egg shells
sewn neatly between the lines with needling pens;
their jagged-edged scrapes like bloodshot eyelids yell
and tooth-on-tooth, like sardined skeletons,
they scream their own forebodance.

We visit them- these words, these muses, masks
that shift and chatter; tectonic plates of insanity
aroused by dreams and loves that would be past
if we'd not brought them with us for posterity ...
to taunt us with some lost pangean essence.

What world was that where we once called our home
and still revolves- slipped into this museum-
convinced we'll keep it safe within these tomes,
defying burial in attic mausoleums?
In reality, we evoked a gestalt monster!

So let the eggs fall, smashing where they lay,
soak yolks with time for yellowing every page,
entomb that glabrous monster though it brays
and use our needling pens in other ways.
If the chicken came first it no longer matters.

Poetic Catharsis

In the words I write others resound-
a half-wit, a scholar, a coursing hound
and the barman who serves them up on ice
never fails to supply my need for one twice.

It's as though he reckons a double-shot's due,
to keep my thirst quenched takes multiple brews
and of what, I ask, as I perch on my stool-
a mother, a lover, an arrogant fool?

They swirl in my mouth, soothed often by lime-
the numbing astringent that coddles my mind
and affords me the time to exact their digestion-
but even yet, I question   I question

What right do they have to invade my senses
and disarm me of all my cultured defenses
by pillaging mores I always held true
until their warping was utterly through?

Once held in a drunken stupor, I
pick up my pen to let them all cry
unabashed and spewed forth for all to see
their cathartic maneuvers imbibed in me!

The barman grins at the rancid pool
and wipes up my counter, clearing the fool,
then serves up more shots as fodder again
for the indomitable stomach of my railing pen!

Onto the Page

When we pry ourselves out and onto the page
we bleed through our fingers and into the pen,

peeling away one more layer of skin
in some perilous effort to feel more sun!

It seems we cannot be uncovered enough
or yet can we open the truths;

The ones that will answer the universe
if, indeed, we might first know the question!

Asunder

She blows in like a gale
        barging past
the doorway of my thoughts—
once neatly assembled
and ready to write,
   now capsized—
            dashed
      asunder
by the whoosh-whir & clatter
of infernal conversation-making
        ... chatter.
            ... chatter.
        ... chatter.
My spirit, once serene,
      churns
like waves of a driving tide,
            curling
         back
upon itself, coiling
   (recoiling)
      in the bantering spray.
No longer adrift
on a recent perspicuity,
      my muse
            & my pen
thrash & flail for a harness—
lovers grappling
            over their lost hold.

Belly-Up

unpumped—
this lollygagged heart refuses
to throb, has turned the pen
belly-up, buried its shale
deep in the briny sea, paled
in its own desire and petrified
with age, petrified to trust love
where love, once penetrated,
oozed ruddily— reckless
in self-abandonment.

The Ivy and Rose

Like the ivy and the rose we climb—
criss-crossing on the trellis,
increasing our own divine entanglement
as we converge and then diverge
in life's continuous grid. Our love
connects in places where we've been,
where we have already bound ourselves
and we are spurred on with each sunrise
to reach out and touch again.

Wintry Shrub

Here we examine the wintry shrub:
a skeletal ghost cloaked
beneath the weight of twinkling ice,
frozen in numb solitude
arbitrary fingers jabbing into
a colder,
more heavy-hearted
air.

A Christmas Mosaic

I.

    december evening—

cloaked by the whiteness
of fresh snowfal, the face-smacking
crisp coldness of an air,

the sweet, heart warming intonement
of Ave Maria playing from a loudspeaker

softly wisps without prejudice
over the red complexion
of homelessness

embodied in subway terminals
and throughout main street alcoves

the full moonlight illuminates
three tattered wise men
hauling newly discarded shipping boxes
from behind a retail store—

christmas gifts
for the princesses of poverty,

perfect mangers
to choke out winter's bite
and nurture true gratitude

through a welcomed sleep
stocked full, overflowing
with sugar plum dreams

drawn vividly
from some bright, wandering star
cast aground

II.
    fragrant gingerbread –

houses decked with snow
and lights, all coloured, twinkle
side by each

the pine and spruce all magical,
dance & echo children's laughter,

play hopscotch with toboggans
on the mottled hillside

while carolers troll the vale
for audience and joiner

churchgoers

dazzling in bright Christmas attire
exchange foyered greetings
and best wishes
in the shadow of a cross

while in the yard, another cross
newly staked
and a widower's tears

ice

III.
    empty stockings
trim the mantle, waiting—

a vibrant fire coughs and crackles,
nudges the fragrance of sweet-charred timber
beyond the hearth's screen.

snowflakes perch in piles
on lattice-worked windows, glisten and bask
in their illuminated warmth then melt away
into the yawning night.

a baby jack scatters paw prints by the woodpile
as a reindeer's hooves mark their place
in a child's visionary landscape.

parents watch a Dickens classic,
sip mugs of hot cider
and entertain a silent war

over the high price of gifting
and who rise first
to wrap.

IV.
   downtown—

storefronts sport sparkling
eye-catching showcases and

in the mall, a child waits;
anticipating that long-awaited moment
of sitting on Santa's knee.

a young man spends his paycheque
to gift a diamond ring, surprise
for the bustling clerk, his girlfriend,
at work two shops away.

Christmas carols pipe through the plaza—

transport a mood of peace, hope and love
among the shopping masses

when interrupted for a news broadcast—
in Afghanistan, six Canadians killed
by a suicide bomber,

seven christs meet Easter early—

& few chance to notice.

This Thieving Flea

Consider the life of this thieving flea
that sucked my blood first and has now drawn yours
without the good manners of preliminary courtship
instilled by our parents as necessities of youth.
Would your mother not consider this sin...
that the flea has pricked her daughter's virgin flesh
and united you and I within its hungry belly
before wedding rites and then, a consummation?
If we kill the flea now do we commit three sins
and murder our three souls together?
... or should we choose to wed the flea too
by consuming it as our first communion?

(reference - "The Flea" by John Donne 1572-1631)

When I am Dead and Buried

My soul will not waste the tears of an abased lover now
but will focus on other fanciful sights
and 'though you heap death wishes upon my brow
I will savour the rest of my renegade life.
When I'm dead and buried, it's then that I will
remember mean wishes and all of that ill-
I'll return to bed you as a ghostly lover,
to incite your passion and build your desire
with unseen hands and face unrecognized
so that when you turn to your chosen spouse
and discover her sleeping like a mouse
your mind will grieve to calm your thighs.
I'll smile at this torment that you'll despise...
that will make you more of a ghost than I!

(reference - "The Apparition" by John Donne 1572-1631)

Of Misfit Hearts

The last time that I died-
and I die every time that you are gone-
having no one to execute my will
I determined that I, myself,
would give you all that I hold of value...
my heart. I wanted you to know
that it was you who had killed me once again.

Yet, even as I reached into my own pale shell
I could not find my loyal heart
where it should have lain
but near that place lay another heart;
composed of a different shade and square-cornered.
Its homage was not singly focused
and clearly I could see it didn't fit.
Suddenly I knew this strange heart's origin
and that it was, indeed,
yours!

(reference - "The Legacy" by John Donne 1572-1631)

Where Does a Falling Star Go?

Where does a falling star go?
Why challenge me to catch one when
you know it burned away? And no,
the child and mandrake root are gone,
the devil's foot been cleft so long
its craftsman's mark has well worn on.
    Mermaids are mute
    and like a brute
their silence you cannot commute.

Clairvoyant ones say this:
a gift like theirs is never
to tell you why you waver
from her to her and kiss to kiss.
The truth, in their perspective, lies
while love's a master of disguise-
    a diamond ring
    needs no bling-
fair women live amongst fair things.

When I find her I'll not tell
instead she'll have my eyes and lips
and every love song ever swelled
will be for me what you'd dismiss.
No wondrous woman true or fair
will nestle you in heaven's hair;
    you will resist
    through every kiss
and always think they don't exist.

(reference - "Go and Catch a Falling Star" by John Donne 1572-1631)

His Own Construction

It's woeful that a learned man
depict conjecture- his brain on hand
    to show him women's attributes
and, instead, paint her indifference;
unworthy of spite or any reverence,
    an object for discarding after use.

To state the visible good of green
as proof that's, in her, left unseen
    rapes her of motherhood virtue
and for contrast he fails to offer shade
of any colour that vices are made.
    His own construction sheds its glue.

Do join me for supper Mr. Donne,
I'm the feast laid out for when you come
    to sate your changing appetite
but as you look upon my table-
if good and bad I am unable-
    then, in me, but a wastrel could delight!

(reference - "Community" by John Donne 1572-1631)

Where the Dream Begins

The world is what it is
        I can't change it alone
and though I pretend to have them yet
        my rose-tint specs left long ago.

I might seem like a dreamer
        seen through my pen
but that is where the dream begins
        and where it ends!

Garment of Lavendar Haze

We stare into the cauldron:
a witches' brew of our own within-ness
simmering in both places at once—
rooted in time yet beyond its depths,
starry skies that twinkle although the twinkling's done
and still, has yet to begin— a visionary dance.

Wizards call us up amid the broth
bubbling, brimming silent in still-too-fresh wonderment
that we've re-turned, as if we were ever gone,
and the lavendar haze that is now our garment
drapes in veils around us, the lightest cloth
that dark can ever touch or think to own.

Here, we come all drawn in-to ourselves
re-membering the mist and all its myst-eries,
solved and dis-solved in this potpourri
of facelessness, passed over for re-lease
to a place where myths and legends ever swell,
made point-device— both real and fantasy.

Northern

The northern lights splay across the horizon,
reach around, outward and span the heights,
even depths of the heavens and shaking
into that cold black, arctic night,
I become witness to great spectral dreams
cradled by a taut landscape—
pulled tight upon an earthy foundation.
I stand here and gaze;
watch shapes rise and shift as if
somehow they are speaking to me
and I would choose
to understand their message.
At times I believe I can.
I can reach out
and they will come to me—
each colour, each brilliant hue
will respond to my bidding,
keening to join every possible vista
of divine Spirit.

The Coyotes' Lament

The snow lies fresh on the ground
and weary— the plodding of coyotes
buried deep up to jointed knees;
their howls make sad, mourning notes.

Winter is always their lean time,
the hibernal prey safely hidden...
but this heavier-blanketed season
has made even the wakeful forbidden.

The grey, muted sky seems unruffled,
as if only I hear their pale voices;
how slow passage breaks their momentum
and alerts their woodland food choices.

Their pleas pull my heart as the sandman
hauls me into a warm, cozy doze
but I wake with the sun and the same song—
the howling of sad, mourning notes.

Defying Convention

You walk on my grave,
your spiked heels digging in,
aerating the lawn, then dancing
into a rapacious Mambo—
You never did know when to quit,

When the mask didn't fit
you didn't care,
   'Love me, love me as I am!'
you laughed and lifted butterfly wings
to a sky too bright for me to follow you
even through a single, thinly-slit eyelid.

And now you return again, unconcerned
about insomnia's side-effects or
my need for beauty sleep.
   'You are most beautiful already!'
you bellow at my monument
   'Rise up you Lazarus, rise up!'

You trample, stomp & scuff up
grass & dirt, shear away my cushion—
unravel the hard-earned quilt of death
skilfully crafted and laid out for me...
so that even now, as I lay in drowsy state,
I remember:

graveyards were always too concrete
to scare you and sunlight, your keeper,
always emanated from your dark pupils
to mystically light the moonless night.
I open my eyes
when you open my casket.

I ask myself
   'Why? Why could you always count on me

to come back at your bidding?
How, through time&time - life&life –
do you always know where to find me?'

That I loved you in life is undeniable:
in death
I set you free!

That you keep digging paths in the gyre,
resurrecting me over&over,
is inexplicably true
devotion.

Ronda Eller aka Wicks
"kinshu ori"

b. 1965 in Toronto, Ontario, Canada

Publishes artwork under her maiden name, Ronda Wicks.
Publishes poetry under her "pen" (married) name, Ronda Eller
and haiku under her haijin name "kinshu ori", which means
"little pen"

Ronda's poetry has been published in Canada and the USA. She is the
National Media Coordinator for the Canadian Poetry Association and
co-owner of participatepoet.yahoogroups.com Ronda is a poetry
publisher, reviewer and competition adjudicator.

http://www.skywingpress.com/rondawicks_eller.html

"SPINNING THE SOUL"

This poetry collection could just as well have been entitled "Spinning the Soul". Poem after poem deals fairly and openly with various vicissitudes of life, drawing the reader in, spinning the soul in surprising directions!

Just as any cycle has its high and low points, so do Eller's poems spin the reader from ebullient enthusiasm to the depth of depression, and back again! She leaves no topic unexamined and wistfully mingles seemingly incompatible ones: In "Au Courant," for example, scientific terms and feelings are woven together seamlessly.

And again, in "Ripple," a wonderfully expressed personal darkness poem, she juxtaposes the anger of smashing dishes with one's place in the universe.

Eller uses various poetic forms, both modern free-verse and some well tried and tested forms. In "Pulled from that Spindled Track" she achieves a beautifully flowing, classical style and captures the fluidity of life then continues her basic theme, the unrelenting spin:

She achieves an utterly beautiful scene in "She speaks to Him of Perfect Union"; another classical style with an abbc rhyme pattern. Here, she achieves an utterly beautiful scene:

*"Oh soul that drifts through moods on open sea
and harbours all its hopes in undertow"*

In "Unzipped Valentine," a playful treatment of Eros and his arrows, Eller fights back as only a poet can, by playing with the word 'quiver': ... *"this year/we quiver..."*

Besides the classical poetic styles, Eller reaches back to Classical and pre-Classical times. In "The Lamentations of Isis," she takes Egypt's primordial myth and conjures up Isis with all her pain of loss within the context of Wisdom. In "Armageddon's Bride," a personality splintered from the Book of Revelations, Eller cleverly shifts from the common people who are the usual victims of Armageddon, to the bride waiting for the "crimson knight", whose touch will *"gain her wisdom."* Eller, like many thinking and feeling people, puts the threat of the Whore of Babylon behind her and recognizes the new feminine principle risen after an age of religious repression.

In "Come My Lover," Eller creates notable lines such as *"You've learned to murmur / recitations of your own rising"* and *"before the morning lifts its lids / and tries to catch us with its glare...."* Jungians will immediately recognize the lifelong dance of the Ego and Animus, a relationship that needs constant work. It is soon followed by "The Alliance ...," another well composed Ego-Animus story, not so veiled this time.

The kingpin or the keystone of this collection is "The Lion and the Golden Calf: A Vision." This is the poem from which the book takes it title. It successfully tackles the immense chasm between Western and Eastern spirituality in four short stanzas, rhyming abba.

In "The Henges' Kiss" Eller continues to spin cycles. In this three part poem, "Lead me to the wood-rot rings" gives us a clue right off that we are dealing with a wood-henge in an abbcca rhyming pattern. In the first part it is the poet who kisses "these timbered feet!" In the second part, about a stone henge, it is still the poet who kisses "those sarsen stones!" In the third and final part, however, the poet lives and dies, "from life to death to life I pass" through cycles of reasonless seasons. Unspoken, the poet establishes the everlastingness of all things with cycles: through her own cycles she makes the henges everlasting as well!

Love and pain, the latter often caused by love, or a lack of it, are recurring cycles in Eller's poetry. In "The Ivy and the Rose" Eller hints that "divine entanglement" may be assured by quantum entanglement, but hopes so is love! Whereas quite a few previous poems dealt with love spurned, here "we are spurred on with each sunrise / to reach out and touch again."

The modern world is also well represented; particularly the pressures and illusions of Christmas. Another 'modern' poem, "Wintry Shrub," is a brief palette of winter reality *"frozen in numb solitude."*

Eller's collection, on the whole, is a wonderful read. She calls upon her muses, Robert Frost, Wm. B. Yeats and John Donne and seamlessly shifts to travels within her soul. Love and loneliness spin along with impertinence and defiance, allowing the reader a variety that is always welcome to make a poetry book readable and valuable.

~ **Daniel Kolos**, Egyptologist, Author, Poet and Documentary Writer. Member of Highway 4 Writers, Words Aloud Poetry Cooperative, The Ontario Poetry Society and the League of Canadian Poets